GET REAL!

The Last Day

by Phil Kettle

Illustrated by
Melissa Webb

Get Real!
The Last Day

Written by Phil Kettle
Illustrations by Melissa Webb
Character design by David Dunstan

Text © 2009 Phil Kettle
Illustrations © 2009 Macmillan Education Australia Pty Ltd

All rights reserved. No part of this publication may be
reproduced, stored in a retrieval system, or transmitted in any
form or by any means, electronic, mechanical, photocopying,
recording, or otherwise, without the prior permission of the
copyright owner. While every care has been taken to trace and
acknowledge copyright, the publishers tender their apologies
for any accidental infringement where copyright has proved
untraceable.

Published by
Macmillan Education Australia Pty Ltd
Level 1, 15–19 Claremont Street, South Yarra,
Victoria 3141
www.macmillan.com.au

Edited by Emma Short

Designed by Jenny Lindstedt,
Goanna Graphics (Vic) Pty Ltd

Printed in China
10 9 8 7 6 5 4 3 2

ISBN: (pack) 9781420278828

ISBN: 9781420278279

Contents

Introduction

The one on the right with a really big smile is Jesse Harrison. The one on the left with a really big smile is Harry Harvard. And the ones standing behind Jesse and Harry and throwing their hats in the air are the rest of the kids in Average Primary School.

So why are they smiling and throwing their hats in the air? Because school has finished for another year, and they're just about to leave Average Primary School for the summer holidays. That means no more school, and no more Principal Dorking or Mrs Payne, for six whole weeks. No wonder everyone is smiling!

Chapter One

The Plan

After spending another average day at Average Primary School, Jesse and Harry would normally hurry home to their tree house on their skateboards. But today was different. Instead of hurrying home to their tree house, Jesse and Harry were hiding in the school library. They were waiting for everyone else in the school to hurry home first.

Jesse and Harry were on a mission. It was the second last day of the school year, and they wanted to make sure that the *last* day of school would be a TOTALLY memorable one. They wanted to fill it with hilarious tricks and side-splitting pranks that were sure to make the students laugh – and the teachers stress.

"I think we should make the last day of school the best day of school in the entire year," said Jesse, stepping out from behind a bookshelf.

"Agreed!" grinned Harry, climbing out of the paper-recycling bin.

Jesse and Harry had come up with a plan that was so hideous, devious and dastardly, it would cause total havoc among the school population. As soon as they were sure that everyone else had left, they raced around the school faster than a speedy mouse being chased by a hungry school cat.

Harry sprayed every blackboard in the school with magic chalk-dissolving spray.

Then Jesse changed the wording on the school sign.

And finally, they drilled small holes in the walls of the mouse house that Mrs Payne's Grade Five class had built at the beginning of the school year.

Harry and Jesse looked over their work and felt very satisfied.

"Well, that's all done then," said Jesse.

"Yes," said Harry. "Tomorrow the fun will begin."

Chapter Two

A Very Short Chapter

A NOTE FROM THE AUTHOR

All readers and fans of Jesse and Harry will know that deep down, Jesse and Harry really are good boys. It's just that sometimes they're a little mischievous. They don't mean any harm with the tricks that they play. They just love having fun.

A WARNING FROM THE AUTHOR

If you (YES, that means **YOU**) think that after reading the rest of this incredible adventure, you might like to play some of the tricks similar to those Jesse and Harry are about to play at Average Primary School — **DON'T**! **Or else you'll be in more trouble than a sleepy chicken trying to cross a busy road.**

Chapter Three

Chips and Peanut Butter

After they finished activating their devious and dastardly plan, Jesse and Harry raced home much faster than a sleepy chicken trying to cross a busy road. They climbed up to their tree house and sat down in their rickety wooden chairs. Then Jesse opened a packet of chips and a jar of peanut butter, and began to talk.

"Tho wot aarr we gointh thoo doo ova thu thumma ollidaiths, Arry?"

"Do you mean 'what are we going to do over the summer holidays, Harry'?" asked Harry.

Jesse stuffed another handful of chips and peanut butter into his mouth – which was already full. "Yeth!" he replied.

"Well, we can have lots of great adventures over summer with our time machine," said Harry.

"Like what?" Jesse asked.

"Well, I've always wondered what it would be like to live in the jungle," Harry said dreamily.

"What sort of jungle?" Jesse asked.

"A big scary jungle somewhere in the middle of Africa...with loads of wild animals. I'd be just like Tarzan!" answered Harry.

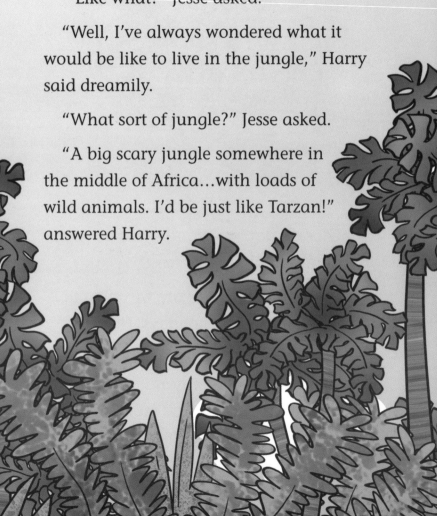

"So Jesse, do you think that we should go back in time to the days of the explorers in deepest darkest Africa, and live with huge and dangerous animals that are very likely to eat us?" asked Harry.

"Well Harry, when you put it like that, NO. I don't want to go to the deepest darkest jungles in Africa," said Jesse.

"Okay, I think I've got another idea," said Harry.

"And what would that be?" Jesse asked.

"I reckon that it would be really cool to go back in time and see what Average was like a long time ago. We might even be able to see what Principal Dorking was like when he was a kid. And then we could try and convince him that he should never become a school principal!"

"Cool, Average Primary School without Principal Dorking...now that's a great idea!" laughed Jesse excitedly.

"But first, we've got tomorrow, the last day of school for the year. AND THAT'S GOING TO BE SO MUCH FUN!" said Harry.

Chapter four

Another Very Short Chapter

A NOTE FROM THE AUTHOR

Question: What do students do when they know they're going home from school for the very last time before the summer holidays begin?

Answer: **They CELEBRATE!**

But first, they have to get through the very last day of school, and now we're going to find out what happened on the very last day of school at Average Primary School.

ANOTHER WARNING FROM THE AUTHOR

Make sure you're lying down before you read the next chapter. If you're not lying down, you might **fall down laughing and hurt yourself**, and that'd be bad — **especially** for you.

Chapter five

The Last Day

The next morning, Jesse and Harry woke
up really early. Normally they were
very late for school because they always
got distracted on the way there, but
not today. Today they were both really
anxious to get to school on time, and so
were the rest of the students at Average
Primary School. That's because Jesse
and Harry had already told them to be
prepared for a day of tricks and laughs
to celebrate the end of the school year.

Meanwhile, Principal Dorking had woken up early too. That was because his dog, Poopeepup, had pulled back the doona and started licking his toes. Poopeepup was reminding Principal Dorking that it was time for their morning walk.

Mrs Payne was also awake. And not only did she wake up early, she woke up with a smile on her face for the first time since the start of the school year! She gobbled down her breakfast and danced out her front gate towards the school.

Because he woke up so early, Principal Dorking arrived at his office much earlier than usual too. But unlike Mrs Payne, Principal Dorking was really sad that it was the last day of the school year.

"Good morning, Principal Dorking! Are you looking forward to the summer holidays?" beamed Mrs Payne, as they passed each other in the corridor.

"It's not a good morning at all, Mrs Payne!" bellowed Principal Dorking. "I hate the summer holidays. In fact, I hate ALL holidays and I even hate weekends!"

When Mrs Payne asked why, Principal Dorking explained further. "Because I don't get to give orders, and I really love giving orders," he said. "Sometimes when I'm on holidays, I try to give my wife orders. That's always bad.

Mrs Dorking refuses to listen to me, and then she refuses to talk to me until the end of the holidays. Actually, that's not always bad!"

Mr Zimmer, the science teacher, had also arrived at school earlier than usual. But unlike Principal Dorking and just like Mrs Payne, Mr Zimmer was really excited about the last day of the school year.

"Good morning! I'm so excited! I think I might even invent something today!" Mr Zimmer said to Mrs Payne and Principal Dorking as he passed them in the corridor. Then he disappeared into the science laboratory.

Talented
Inventor
at work
DO NOT DISTURB

Mr Zimmer staggered out of the science laboratory and past Principal Dorking's office. His hair was standing up on end and his eyebrows had been completely blown off.

"Hmmm, I guess you'd call that a failure," said Principal Dorking, looking up from his desk.

But Mr Zimmer was still excited. He may have just blown up the science laboratory, but as soon as the day was over, he would be flying across the country to a very important science conference. At this conference, Mr Zimmer was going to work together with a team of very talented science teachers to create a unique chemical formula. This formula would be used to create a special spray that could vaporise problem students forever!

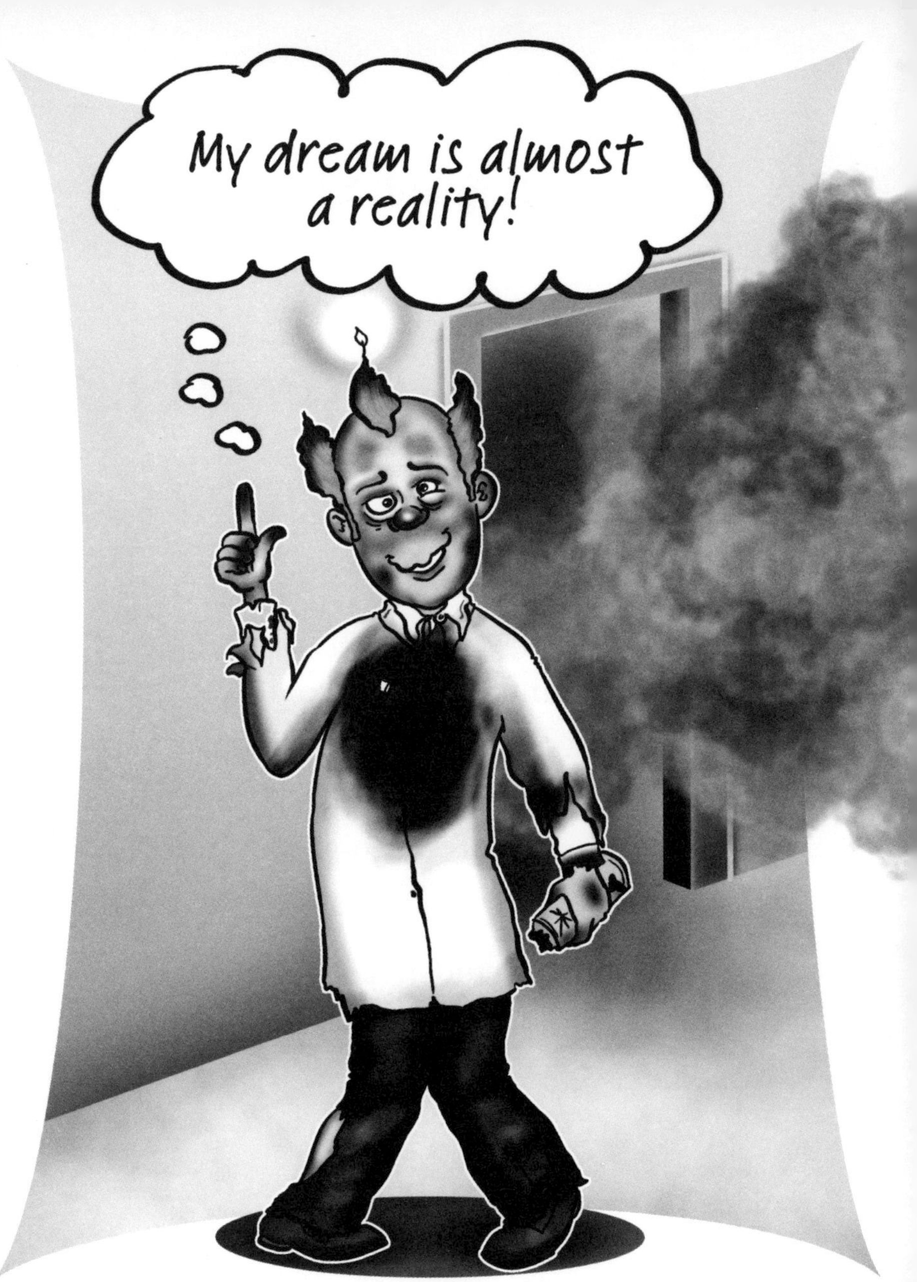
My dream is almost a reality!

Chapter Six

The Final Assembly

When Harry and Jesse arrived at Average Primary School, Principal Dorking was standing at the school gates, welcoming all his loyal students for the last time before the summer holidays.

"Don't be sad, students. I know you'll miss me...but I'll be here when you come back next year!"

Harry and Jesse smiled at Principal Dorking.

"We hope you have a nice day," they said together.

"Hmmm," thought Principal Dorking, eyeing the boys suspiciously. "Why don't you boys spend the summer holidays seeing how far you can walk – preferably away from Average!"

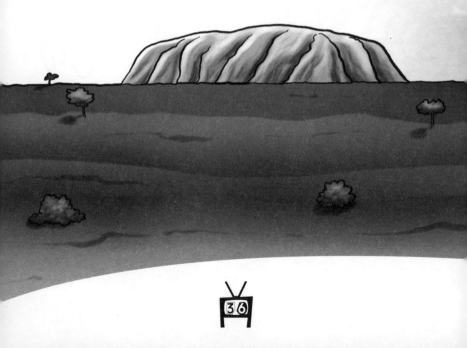

The students and teachers assembled in the school hall for the last time that year. Principal Dorking prepared to address the entire school.

"Average teachers and students," he announced, after clearing his throat. "Today is the last day of school before the summer holidays begin. If you're feeling really sad like me, then please raise your hands."

tap tap tap

Principal Dorking tried again. "Well then, if any students would like to keep coming to school during the holidays, please raise your hands. Except for Jesse Harrison and Harry Harvard, who are totally banned from coming anywhere near me or the school outside official school hours."

Still no hands were raised. Principal Dorking tapped the microphone. "Hmmm, mustn't be working properly," he said quietly. "I must remember to get a new one next year."

Chapter Seven

Mayhem

Soon after the assembly had finished, but not as soon as most people in the school hall would have liked, the students and teachers returned to their classrooms. When Mrs Payne reached the Grade Five classroom, she had hoped to find all her students sitting quietly at their desks.

Mrs Payne was in such a good mood that she ignored the total mayhem unfolding before her. "I'm so pleased that today is the last day of the school year," she said happily to any student that would listen. "If any of you want to move to another school during the holidays, I'd be very happy to help you pack up your desks."

Then Mrs Payne whistled a happy tune and declared that she was looking forward to a long and happy summer holiday at her very favourite beach resort.

Just at that moment, Principal Dorking tapped on the classroom door and coughed loudly. Mrs Payne rushed outside into the corridor and discussed something quietly with Principal Dorking. When she returned, she wasn't very happy at all.

"I'd like to advise that next year,
I won't be teaching Grade Five," she said
in a low voice.

GREAT! HOORAY! AWESOME!

"I'll be teaching Grade Six instead,"
she finished quietly.

BOO! MOAN! OH NO!

A few minutes later, when everyone had recovered from this shocking news, Mrs Payne decided to get the class back under control. She stood up, grabbed some chalk and scribbled furiously on the blackboard.

GRADE FIVE STUDENTS MUST BEHAVE

OR ELSE!

Then she turned and faced the class. "Now students, I want you to read what I've written on the blackboard and then DO IT!"

Jesse and Harry started to snigger.

"But Mrs Payne," said Lenny 'the Stink' Edwards. "There's *nothing* written on the blackboard."

Mrs Payne turned and looked at the blank blackboard. She scratched her head, picked up the chalk and wrote on the blackboard again.

"Now students," she continued. "I really do expect you to do exactly as I've written on the blackboard for the rest of the school day."

**GRADE FIVE STUDENTS
MUST BEHAVE
OR ELSE!**

But as soon as Mrs Payne had turned back towards the class, the writing on the blackboard had vanished again.

AUTHOR NOTE

Of course, we all know the reason why the writing on the blackboard kept disappearing. Mrs Payne didn't.

"But Mrs Payne," said Harry, trying to stop himself from laughing.

"There's nothing on the blackboard," finished Jesse, trying not to look guilty.

Mrs Payne turned and looked at the blackboard again, but the boys were right. There was no writing on it at all. She punched her desk with frustration. That made Jesse and Harry laugh so hard that they nearly fell off their chairs.

As the rest of the class joined in the laughter, Mrs Payne suddenly noticed an empty can of magic chalk-disappearing spray in the waste-paper bin under her desk.

Mrs Payne was so angry, she thumped her head against the blackboard three times! When she turned back to face the class, there seemed to be twice as many students as usual. Even worse, there seemed to be twice as many Jesses and Harrys too. Poor Mrs Payne screamed, then fainted clean away.

Chapter eight

Meanwhile...

...outside the classroom, a series of incredibly unbelievable events were unfolding.

The mice that lived in the mouse house had finally discovered the tiny holes in the walls of their home. One hundred and thirty-seven little white mice were scurrying in all different directions, happily exploring the school.

Principal Dorking was up on a ladder,
trying to fix the school sign. Suddenly
a little white mouse ran up the ladder,
up his trousers, across his head and
back down his trousers again. Principal
Dorking lost his balance, went flying off
the ladder and hit the ground hard.

Samantha Smithers opened her locker
in the corridor outside her classroom
and a tiny white mouse jumped out.
She dropped her books and screamed.

eeeeeeeeeeeeeeeeeeeeee
EEEEEEEEE
EEEEEEK!

Lenny 'the Stink' Edwards opened his lunchbox and discovered a tiny white mouse eating its way through his sandwiches.

Rocky Rockman noticed a tiny white mouse scurrying across the classroom floor and jumped up on top of his desk.

Jesse and Harry were still sitting at their desks. They were laughing and smiling and listening to the lovely sound of chaos echoing all around them.

"I told you today was going to be the funniest day of the year," Harry giggled.

"You're not wrong there, Harry!" chuckled Jesse.

Chapter Nine

But Then...

…Mrs Payne looked up from under her ice pack and saw Jesse and Harry laughing. She glared at them with piercing eyes, her head throbbing and her blood beginning to boil. Jesse and Harry looked at each other and silently decided it was time they were somewhere else – anywhere but Mrs Payne's Grade Five classroom. The boys shot out the door as fast as they could, with Mrs Payne in hot pursuit.

Out the front of the school, Principal Dorking had finally managed to get up on his feet, but he was pretty sure he had a broken leg. Suddenly he saw two boys running out the school gates, their skateboards tucked tightly under their arms.

Then he saw Mrs Payne running after the two boys, closely followed by Lenny 'the Stink' Edwards, Samantha Smithers and Rocky Rockman at the back of the pack. "Harvard and Harrison!" he bellowed, and then he decided to join the chase.

Jesse and Harry raced home faster than one hundred and thirty-seven tiny white mice being chased by a very hungry school cat. As they crossed Average Park, they jumped on their skateboards and left the rest of the pack behind. When they reached the big tree that separated their backyards, they jumped off their skateboards and scrambled up the ladder to their tree house.

"That was so much fun! I could do it all over again," puffed Harry.

"I reckon! What an awesome day!" huffed Jesse.

"Are you thinking what I'm thinking?" winked Harry.

"I think I very well might be," laughed Jesse, and he programmed their destination into the time machine.

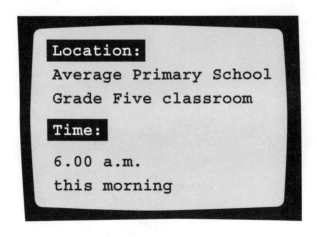

Location:
Average Primary School
Grade Five classroom

Time:
6.00 a.m.
this morning

"Ready, Harry?" asked Jesse.

"Ready, Jesse!" Harry nodded.

Together they put their hand on the red button to activate the time machine.

"One…two…THREE!"

In a blur of dust and a rush of imagination, they disappeared into the recent past.

Harry and Jesse found themselves back in their beds. The sun was just coming up and it was the last day of the school year before the summer holidays. They were both really anxious to get to school on time, and so were the rest of the students at Average Primary School. That's because Jesse and Harry had already told them to be prepared for a day of tricks and laughs to celebrate the end of the school year…

A QUESTION FROM THE AUTHOR

I WONDER WHAT HAPPENS NEXT?

The End

Let's Write

Keeping It Interesting

The words you choose to write your story with, and the way you write them, are really important. Using colourful language really helps to keep your readers interested. For example, imagine if I wrote the first paragraph of Chapter Nine like this:

But Then...

> Mrs Payne looked up. She saw Jesse and Harry. She looked at them. Her head hurt. Jesse and Harry looked at each other. They decided to leave the classroom. They ran outside. Mrs Payne followed them.

Not very interesting, is it? Turn back to page 55 of this book to see how descriptive language can bring your story to life!

My story plan – descriptive language

So open up your creative-writing book and start thinking about all the colourful and exciting ways you might describe your characters or locations. Make a list of common words like 'run' or 'said' or 'fast'. Then make another list of uncommon words that you might use instead – like 'scamper', 'gallop', 'sprint', 'shouted', 'suggested', 'replied', 'quick' or 'like lightning!'

Make sure that you add to your lists whenever you hear or read some great descriptive language. And remember:

Interesting Words = Interested Readers!

Jesse and Harry Present

About the Author

Jesse: Now Phil, I reckon that if you ever did anything at school like Harry and I did in this story, then you wouldn't be here to tell the tale!

Phil: Jesse, I reckon you might be right.

Jesse: So Phil, where did you get the idea for this story?

Phil: The idea for this story came from something that I saw.

Jesse: You mean that you actually saw a school where someone did some of the things that happened in this story?

Phil: Well, actually no. I saw a movie where something happened just like in this story.

Jesse: What was the name of the movie?

Phil: Can't remember.

About the Illustrator

Harry: *Hey Melissa, did you ever do anything bad when you were at school?*

Melissa: *I didn't think it was THAT bad.*

Harry: *What was your favourite subject?*

Melissa: *I really liked music (art too).*

Harry: *I bet you always got an A+ in art class!*

Word-up!

Medical staff: a doctor's cane

Morbid: a higher offer than the first bid in an auction

Outpatient: a person who has fainted

Recovery room: a place to do upholstery

Tablet: a small table

A Laugh a Minute!

What is the fastest fish in the water?
A motor pike!

Who is the biggest gangster in the sea?
Al Caprawn!

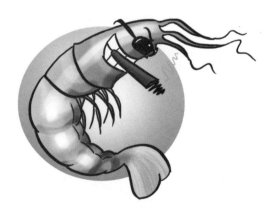

Why did the banana snore?
Because it wanted to wake up the rest
of the bunch!

What is green with four legs and two trunks?
Two seasick tourists!

Why is perfume so obedient?
Because it is scent wherever it goes.

*How many rotten eggs does it take to make
a stink bomb?*
Quite a phew!

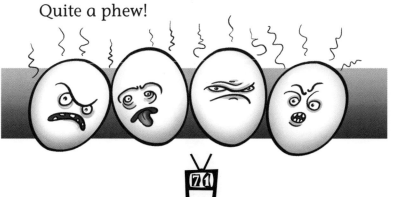

Other Titles in the Series